A Slow Education

A Slow Education

Poems

David Giver

A Slow Education

Copyright © 2013 by David Giver

Published by Shabda Press
P.O. Box 70483
Pasadena, CA 91117
www.shabdapress.com

All rights reserved. No part of this book may be reproduced or transmitted in any form or by any means without written permission of the author.

ISBN 978-0-9853151-2-2

To all those that love me ....
especially mog & srgo

Contents

Memoir 1

1

A Proper Eulogy 5
Our Little Piece of America, in Germany 7
"Grandma, you smell like smoke" said the birthday girl 9
I Like To Recall the First Time I Witnessed Life 11
"Did your mother teach you that?" inquired Ruby 13
I Have Never Seen My Father Cry 14
A Daily Suicide 16

2

Indoctrination 19
Look At the Pheasant 20
Reveille 22
Confederacy 23
A Gentle Reminder 24
My Dreams Of Nigeria 26
The One I Pushed Away 28

3

The Master Insistent 31
Tahara 32
Out of Love 33
If I Forget You, O Yerushalayim 35
Pharaoh 36
Day of Atonement 38

4

Remember, Do Not Forget 43
Gracious 44
Gone is the Beat of Your Heart 47

Lost	48
Best Left Unanswered	49
To My Daughter on Her Death	50
If Only Amnesia	51
There is No Term for Parents That Lose a Child	52

5

Occupation Forces	55
This Is How I Know That I Love You	57
Coup d'état	58
No More a Useful Man	59
Foreclosure On My Mother's Uterus	60
If Only I Could Procrastinate My Death	61
All I Wish I Needed In Life	62

Memoir

My youth is like
the old pull knob
cigarette machine,

gone. I do not
really remember
either well.

My youth is all
pictures in albums and
stories told by
parents who lived

them, so real are
they that I can't
sort out the facts
from the

myths in my
own life. I search
for the meaning
in a life

that I am
trying to make
my own.

1

A Proper Eulogy

I thought he was just asleep
so still, frozen in what I
later learned was a coffin

I was only five, what did I
know. Dressed in clothes that looked bought
for just such an occasion.

I had never seen him in
a suit. To be honest I
had only ever seen him

in plaid shirts, work pants and the
Carolina Cocks mesh hat
that he always wore. Standing

next to the pine casket was
an old man who could not be
bothered to show emotion.

He spoke of my grand father
in the most generic of
terms, so obviously a

script. I turned to my mom to
ask if I was right, she just
cried. Even I knew that he

deserved more. An addiction
to tobacco is what killed
him, but not what defined him.

A Slow Education

He was a Southerner, a
South Carolina man who
worked for the railroad of

Michigan, following a
woman he loved only when
she was unavailable

to him. A father to six
of whom my mother was the
baby. Her memories of

a man much beyond his prime.
Trying to keep up his looks
as they began to fall by

the wayside. To her he was
a gentle Goliath. A
different man from his youth

when he held the world by its
balls and his word was the end
of all arguments at home.

His youth had made a mark that
was hard to wash away, but
he tried. No longer the drunk,

no longer the husband, no
longer the father to six,
he was the man that she loved.

David Giver

Our Little Piece of America, in Germany

I scurried down the
stairs
of our third
floor
government issue
walkup and

leapt past the
kids at play
on the stoop
and out into the
irradiated
clouds

of Chernobyl.
My lungs filled
with the crisp
spring air of
Germany as I

realized my mother
was right, it was
way too cold out
to be in shorts,
but there I was
building sandcastles

among
the metal slides
and jungle
gyms of my
youth.

A Slow Education

We had been
promised,
or at least told by
the nice man in
uniform on the television,
that the sand

was safe and
we believed him even
after the local kids
at the school told
us that they could
no longer play in their
own sandboxes
just beyond
our complex

and sure enough
they were right, for
at summer's end
the sand was
replaced.

"Grandma, you smell like smoke" said the birthday girl

The girl was only four
and after all
it was her birthday, but

Ruby never forgave her.
She never forgave
anyone. She sure never
forgave her husband
for dying on her while
she was pregnant with
their fourth son, and she
was never going to forgive
this grandchild,

throwing the
charge back in her
face at the kid's
fifth, sixth and
seventh birthdays.

At every birthday
until Ruby was no
longer invited to
birthdays.

each time with the claim
that it was a lie,
that someone else,
the mom maybe,
was the one guilty

and yet always found
among the things in
Ruby's purse were
the remains of at least
one pack of Virginia Slims.

David Giver

I Like To Recall the First Time I Witnessed Life

A borrowed second grade
classroom, as

I was just
a visitor,

a migrant.
This was the

second of
three schools I

would frequent
that year.

And it was the
best of the three.

It had eggs
enshrined in glass

that one day just
exploded one by one

into tiny bundles
of feathers.

Each spring I
relive this moment

by going down
to the farm and

A Slow Education

garden store around
the corner

and finding the metal
tub filled to capacity

with brand new
baby chicks

alive just like they
were so many years ago.

David Giver

"Did your mother teach you that?" inquired Ruby

My grandmother's
name was Rebecca
but everybody called
her Ruby.

I guessed it was for
the red color
that her hair
once held,

but I never
dared to ask; as
such was the fear
of the summer
that I lived
in her nearly
empty existence

of reading the National
Enquirer and watching
reruns of Perry Mason
and Simon & Simon.

I Have Never Seen My Father Cry

He teared up
once in a fit
of rage

the first time
he came to pick
up my sister
and me after the
separation,
that would end
in divorce.

Being naïve
I mistook it
for crying and
asked him about
it, I was told
he never
cried.

I cry. I remember
my first memory
of crying; my father
caused it.

I had asked why my mom
had not yet come
home from work and when
would we be eating dinner.

Only to be told
that she was probably
out fucking her boyfriend.

That was the first time
my father had made
me cry, at least
that I could recall.

A Daily Suicide

His newly masculine hands
ran through the
slight curls of
my hair

as he made me submit
to mock forced fellatio
and told me
how I would love him
for it.

I begged
for him
to stop
my pub(l)ic humiliation

but all that my plea
could do was hang
itself from the door
frame of the bathroom
stall.

2

David Giver

Indoctrination

      A low pitched voice comes on
      over the speakers of the
      bus and goes on and on about
      how we are about to become men.
      I am not paying close attention
      as I try to make out the black horizon

      and our place upon it.
      A hulking figure appears
      in a freshly starched
      uniform and we step off
      into our new environs,

      banks of phones crowd
      a room off
      the main hall. I dial,
      but still
      no one is home.

      I am third in line for a cut
      from the first shift barber and then
      fitted for my size 8
      and a half running shoes.

      I am not a man. I am a number.

      I hurry
      and wait
      for my naval
      career
      to end.

Look At the Pheasant

My dad has worn
glasses since the
first grade, my
mom since the third

and somehow I had
made it 'til I was
nineteen, but all
good things come
to an end

I, too, would need to
wear glasses

the Navy doc was
quick and to the
point

"one or two, which looks best"

"one"

"you said two the last time"

"sorry, two"

"which is it?"

"I don't know"

"damn it, let me look at your eyes,
look over at the pheasant"

David Giver

I did not know what
to do, I did not know
what a pheasant was,
and too proud to ask

I just looked around
the room until he
began to scream at
me.

And that was it
exam done.

A week later, I could
see with my pair
of thick, black plastic
glasses.

Reveille

No more would I shower in a crowd of men,
cracking jokes as I stood
bare ass
waiting my turn,
averting my eyes
to prove that I was not gay
and that I only had eyes
for the ladies.

No longer would I have
to sleep in the bunk
beds, as far as the eye
could see, in hopes that
the kid on the top bunk
would not piss his pants
at night in an attempt
to be sent home.

No more would I have to
eat the assembly line
meals of the mess hall,
all the time on the look
out for bad meat.

No longer was I at boot camp.
I was finally free,
or so I thought,
as I took my seat
on the plane and closed
my eyes.

Confederacy

Old, negro women
with hands worn thin
from palmetto fronds,
weaving a living
off the guilt
of foreigners.
Profits made
from rehabbed slave markets.
I wilt
in the South's,
winter sun.

Air filled with the
scent of pralines and rebellion,
as my Northern air
invades the South.

Decadent and deliberate,
Southern diction,
broad avenues of time through
which I wander,
daring to grasp; pride,
pomp
and circumstance
of war.

A Gentle Reminder

I stood still, trying
not to move
a muscle

the hope being that
maybe I could
just up and
disappear

but my heart gave me away

I was sure that he
could hear it

it felt as though
it was about
to break
through my chest
and fall, silenced,
to the floor

the command master
chief's office smelled
of hate
covered up by
cologne

I recall his face and
how it turned all so
many shades of red
as his rage took over
my life

David Giver

much of what
he said has
left me, but
I still carry the
fear in me of
the toothless

grin on the face
of the sailor that he
said was to be my boss

and how I would
wake each day to
paint the ship that
I had been trained for
so long to sail.

I still hate him for what
he did that day

as I have yet to
be able to
walk out of
that office.

My Dreams Of Nigeria

He stood six and
one half feet tall
and I at five
foot three

an odd couple
to say the
least
his skin – a

mix of Africa
and Montana and
I the pale hue
of the British

isles
twins, we were
not
Eugene was the
one friend I
could be
sure to count
on

and it was to him
I wrote my
suicide notes
those short, vague

David Giver

looks into the
life that I
wanted to
cease –

it was Eugene
that talked me
out of the bottle
of pills I
was holding

and it was in his room
that I slept
as he watched over me
until I could get help

I don't know
Eugene anymore

after those
days ended and
I went home
we lost touch,
but it is
to him
that my daughter
owes her life.

The One I Pushed Away

Life mars the face
of my first love
in her attempt
to cheat time.

More and more becomes
revealed in this ugly
morose
parade.

She labors past me
with all of the grace
of an elephant, trying

to show me
how wrong I was
to leave her.

Her thinning hair
pulled back and
bound, eyes painted
blue, looking

more like a grandmother
than the twenty-
something she is

and all I can do
is think how lucky
I am to have cut
my loses years
ago.

3

David Giver

The Master Insistent

The world
confines
my l-rd,

good or bad,
in a
prison.

O G-d,
king of
substance,

we
wait upon you.

Tahara

An angelic being
vulnerable, nude
abandoned.

A roadmap of life
and disease
stiffened
stoic

waters rushing over
cleansing
anew

shrouded in the garb
of the molochim

buried under the
dust of man
awaiting redemption

Out of Love

"... and that man was sincere and upright,
g-d fearing and shunning evil." Iyov 1:1

If only I could be like Iyov
to suffer with no complaint,
to lose with no loss.

If I have even the
slightest problem
I am the first
to complain, to bitch,
to tell everyone
(of how I have been
wronged. How I had
to live through the
pain of a pregnancy
that seemed to be filled
with every obstacle
out there. To be
told that we were
to have twins ... but
they are in the same sack
and there was a chance that
they could strangle each other
if their cords tangle ... but
they have twin to twin
transfusion syndrome, one
fetus is killing itself
to try to feed its blood to
the other ... but
one of them did not make it
through surgery)

of my woe so
that I can be
given their sympathy,
their love; to be
wanted, even pitied.

If I suffer loss (and
I have)
I become lost,
given over to my
sadness, a
being beyond
help, unable to cope.

If only I could be like Iyov.

If I Forget You, O Yerushalayim

I stand
erect,
trembling.

I see g-d.
I feel him before me,
but I know it is a dream,
as I will always be a tourist,

until
moshiach comes;
may he not take
too long.

Pharaoh

I dwell in Egypt
or is it Mitzrayim,
either way, I am
a slave.

I live
in constant fear
of myself and
how I work so
hard toward the failure
of my marriage.

I am
consumed by
thoughts and dreams
of the naked
bodies of just about
every woman I meet
and how inadequate
these thoughts make me
seem, when even there,
in my own mind, I
am not virile and I under-
perform.

I am not even the
Hero
of my own
dreams, leaving that
role to the man

David Giver

that bursts through the
wall of the room
to take my place
in bed.

I fall
further each day,
and beg to be raised
to be forgiven
and yet know
full well

that the next
day will prove
to be more
of the same.

I dwell in Egypt
or is it Mitzrayim.
either way, I am
a slave.

Day of Atonement

I stand before you
stripped of my
façades

wincing at the
fact that you
know of my lust
for my next door
neighbor, Mrs.
(nevermind, you
know the one)

and how I try
to find ways
to escape my
daughter's cries,
to leave such
jobs to my wife
even though she
may need the sleep

or reprieve
more than I.
I know that I
cannot escape
you, but damned
if I do not try
to. My broken,

naked, body

huddled
in an attempt
to disappear.

I have tried
to reason away
your omniscience,
to believe I was
hidden and that you
would not find me.

I was
wrong.
I beg of
you,
I plead with
you,
forgive me.

4

David Giver

Remember, Do Not Forget

Tears stream
down the topography of my face,
as my hopes for children,
like salmon swim
and jump against the current,
with the sole desire to go home
to spawn.

Alas they fail,
and end their days,
smashed against the rocks.

Gracious

Old Victorian home of doctor's
        office, wainscoting on the walls
        of semi-modern exam table
        and cold stirrups.

We knew (of course we knew) one
        week had passed, we were
        sure of conception.

Blood test results of numbers
        racing up the charts, a bit
        too high.

I never know what to look for
        on these images of life,
        still life, not in colour;

"there they are", "what do you
        mean they?" those high numbers
        not for waste, twins.

"those two circles, rings" twins,
        double strollers and money
        out of the pocket
        of the evening shift.

Threatened by a drunken Bosnian
        gangster or was it the late
        night currency trader
        from Copenhagen, chain smoking
        coffee breaks on the yen.

David Giver

Big bellied concerns realized
        and diagnosed and far away
        Rhode Island bound and Brown

admitted it was true but not
        conclusive third opinion or
        second first opinion. Depart
        free clinic odor of complacency.

"why the fuck did I need to take
        a day off for this" 2 p.m.
        5 o'clock shadow and
        asked me of my origin

"vermont", "for this." I asked myself
        the same question, only five
        in the nation and we get the
        one operating out of
        a free clinic.

Machine assisted family support
        structure and $200 a night
        double beds of accepted
        and free mason graffiti.

Multi-domed trek through dark
        streets while room service
        brought milk.

I drank at some low occupancy
        sports bar trying to remember
        to forget.

A trip home, work and again back
        to Rhode Island as this time
        is different, worse,
        with a need for miracles.

A Slow Education

Success, death and breakfast
> forceps training and no time to
> cry.

No outlet just silent screams
> to G-d of grief and
> thanks as you were not
> alone and neither was I.

No hope, just possible burial all
> based on whether or not
> she came out with the looks
> of a baby, or just a clump,
> a ball, of cells. She was the
> latter.

Medical school seclusion and
> lack of bedside manner with
> questions of need to fill out
> a death certificate.

Here I am explaining to almost
> twenty years of education that
> nineteen weeks comes before
> twenty.

You are gone but I am still asked to
> pick up your remains. Speechless
> again, I refuse and now I sit and
> wonder if a granite finish
> might have been more appropriate.

I think of you, know you, and speak to you,
> receive from you great love in
> knowing that your mother and
> I were your choice, if not
> accomplished.

Davia Giver

Gone is the Beat of Your Heart

yet you are still there.
We check for your twin;
alive.

Your mother turns away.
I am her watchman,
letting her know when she can turn back.

You are buried behind your sister.
A daughter who
haunts our future
and how do we tell her

that you have died.
We hope that
she will just know

and that our words
just explain away
that empty feeling
inside.

Lost

    I remember the rhythm of your heart
    that repetitive thump
    echoing through the room

    your frame
    coming into focus on our
            black and white screen.
    How the doctor pointed out your landmarks
            and that which made you a woman
    and how we pleaded for your life

    and then you were ...

Best Left Unanswered

What can I do?

You are dead,
but your twin still
thrives inside your
mother's full womb.

She glows as does the no vacancy sign
by the side of the road, allowing
the traveler no reprieve.

And how do we
explain our joy
in the face of
so much grief?

To My Daughter on Her Death

I try to waste away

to defy the day
I saw you
dead,

and all I can do
is apologize,

and let you know
that I begged and
pleaded with G-d
for it to be me

not you.

I begged that I die
in your place. That
you be given a chance
to live, to see
the world.

I have seen the
Alps, Buckingham
Palace, Templo
Mayor and the Rio
Magdalena.

And what have you
had the chance
to see?

If Only Amnesia

The joy of new life,
your tiny fingers wrapped
in a fist around my pinky,
your eyes closed tight,
fast asleep,
in the crook of my arm.
I look down at you
and smile because I
know that your blood
is my blood, that you
are the only thing that
now matters to me. I
love you.

Gone, lost, is
your sister
as though
strewn by the side of the road
among the cigarette butts
and wildflowers

among the feelings
I try so hard to forget,
but can't help but
remember.

There is No Term for Parents That Lose a Child

Our hearts
like fall's fallen leaves
crushed under foot,

a loud music
out of respect
for the dead,

never again
to be whole
as we slow the flow of emotions,

and begin
the search
for our belongings among the mire.

5

Occupation Forces

    Glacial ice
    gives way to
    thick, black mud
    of spring.

    Neighborhood cats again
    make a home under my front porch.

    A behemoth in furs,
    with a slow
    pregnant gait, comes to rest,

    as the others
    hold daily turf wars over
    my patio set

    and I
    scheme of ways to
    rid myself
    of these squatters.

    Yet
    I fear the very real
    consequences of such
    actions.

    So
    at night
    I dream of
    one day going
    to Wal-Mart
    and buying
    a pellet gun,

taking aim on my
front porch and
putting my foe
to death.

David Giver

This Is How I Know That I Love You

I awake to your
knee in my back
and an absence of
blankets.

I turn over and almost
fall from the bed.

I try to move close
to you
but I can't
manage to sleep
amongst your hair.

Sleep fleeting,
I awake to
your snoring

and await the
break of
day.

Coup d'état

>Rule over
>my own life
>is being challenged
>by a small child.
>
>She will one day
>succeed, soon I am
>afraid, and in
>doing so begin
>to drown me
>
>in a vast ocean of
>skinned knees, broken
>bones, coming of age,
>boyfriends/girlfriends,
>experimentation,
>etc…

David Giver

No More a Useful Man

We sit and learn
"one foot; two feet"
am I even teaching you
or am I just bringing
back to you
the knowledge of
    your birth.

Your mutters are
    now sentences.
Your thoughts are
    now actions.

Soon,
you will stop being
my little girl.

Soon,
you will be
a woman.

Foreclosure On My Mother's Uterus

A house, not
a home

a rental from
which I

was forcibly
removed,

three weeks
late,

and now is
listed for

demolition, due
to faulty

plumbing.
The last

constant in
my fractured

life
is gone.

David Giver

If Only I Could Procrastinate My Death

Each beat of my heart
feels as though it is removed,
as are the dates,
from the calendar
that is my life.

All I Wish I Needed In Life

She smiles slightly
as her arms wrap
around me

squeezing me
as though this
is our final
goodbye

as though
the day is still
miraculous to
her and she
does not know
that it will
be back again
tomorrow.

www.ingramcontent.com/pod-product-compliance
Lightning Source LLC
LaVergne TN
LVHW091319080426
835510LV00007B/559